SO TELL ME . . . WHO AM I?

SO TELL ME . . . WHO AM I?

CBDOWNEY

To order additional copies of this book, contact:
Xlibris Corporation
1-888-795-4274
www.Xlibris.com
Orders@Xlibris.com
103577

INTRODUCTION

We all know who we are and how we think. There's no mystery in that. There is, however, a mystery in what the seemingly common objects that we subconsciously encounter and use on an everyday basis would think or say if it were possible for them to do so.

This book, unscientifically, allows those objects to do just that. Objects from our everyday surroundings will attempt to communicate to you; to explain what they are and what they do. It's at this point that you may very well realize how little thought you've ever given to those objects even though many of them are absolutely a part of your everyday encounters.

Those objects, within their own three to four paragraph descriptive point-of-views, will try to get you to guess who they are. You'll surely find that you knew them all along.

So . . . in which paragraph will you be able to answer their question: **"Who Am I?"**

Thank you, Gina and Megan, for

tolerating me while I stayed so

involved with this book.

Believe me, I *do* appreciate

your patience.

Carl

WHO AM I?

Wanna trade places with me? Think about it; people come from miles around just to see me! Actually, I don't suppose they're necessarily coming to see me but rather coming to see what happens to me out there! Before you answer, hear me out.

Those who pay to see me, so to speak, may get to touch and even keep me, if they're lucky enough to have me come their way. If that happens they'd better be ready because I'll be coming fast and hard! However, I don't think that's what they paid for. I think they paid to see how I get handled . . . 'out there'.

'Out there', several individuals are assembled on a green expanse and while one from that group is slinging me with all his might at someone, that same someone is trying to beat me with a stick. When I do get smacked around, the guys 'out there' will scramble to pick me up.

Sometimes, if I get whacked hard enough, it will awe the viewers, and those on that green expanse will race full speed in an attempt to cradle me into their soft, leathery, flexible device. If they're successful they'll leisurely return me to one of their colleagues until I'll finally reach a certain centrally located one who, again, will sling me toward another who will also try to beat me with *his* stick!

Occasionally, one of those 'stick' guys will send me far enough that I'll end up with those sometimes joyous subjects way out there. When that happens, those individuals will also scramble to get to me, sometimes spilling things and knocking others out of their way while trying to get me to settle into their outstretched hands.

I'm a little resentful of those who have become legendary at my expense. All eyes were on *me*, after all! *I'm* the one that went that far and made that bevy of viewers roar with approval! *I* deserve the credit!

I guess you're wondering why I would want to trade places with anyone when I'm having such a 'ball'.

Who Am I?

Who Am I?

I sometimes wonder what this world is coming to. I mean, you guys have been here for thousands of years; not as long as me but still, thousands of years! Oh, you've improved. You've adapted. Apparently you have a decent sized brain and have continually put that brain to use in order to better yourselves.

So why then, are you continually returning to the world that you worked so hard from which to remove yourselves? You began as a tiny living thing and eventually adapted to the point where you could leave your 'old' environment and be away from any involvement with me. You adapted to a dryer lifestyle and you know what? That's all right with me because I'm where I want to be. This is what I was given; this is what I am! I'm designed to constantly be on the move, to search, to hunt, to kill, to eat! It's what I do AND-I-LOVE-IT! I've been doing it for millions of years!

Therefore, knowing what it is that I do, why are you so appalled when I do it? I'm doing nothing to bother you in your world so why bother me in mine? Why should you have a death wish out for me and mine? Oh, yes. Most of you do think that we should be killed, especially after that contrived, theatrical attempt some years back that made me and mine all seem like monsters. After that worldwide character assassination everyone was afraid to go to the beaches for fear of being the ones who would 'turn the sea red'!

You've abducted some of us and placed us inside gigantic, see-through containers where you and yours can stop by to stare at us in absolute amazement and, in absolute safety. We haven't come this far to be your 'freak show'! We're living creatures, just as you are, continually trying to find ways to survive. We just wish you'd allow that to be.

We each have a domain. Why don't you wade out here a little farther and see who **this** one belongs to.

Who Am I?

Who Am I?

I'm one of those lonesome souls who takes a lot of crap from people. Their use of me means they are attempting to be neat. They're trying to show themselves, and anyone else, that they are cognizant of the fact that everything has a place and if they follow that premise they will be looked upon as optimally organized, civilized, and . . . sanitary!

That's all well-and-good for them but what would one think of me? I mean, tossing me all the stuff they don't want; never seeming to care if I want it or not! And what do I do about it? Nothing! Nothing but just stand there and take it! Oh, every once in awhile it gets to the point where they know that "I've had it up to here" and that I just won't take anymore!

Sometimes they'll call on Little Billy, from upstairs, to take me out and give my stuff to a bigger one of me. That little dude is rough on me though! If my stuff doesn't come out of me easily, Little Billy will slam me against the sides of the bigger me until I have nothing left! I think it angers him a little when my stuff won't come out.

He will then bring me back in and someone will wipe me down in order to remove some of the substances that are adhering to my surfaces. (I'll admit, I do get pretty 'icky' at times.) But wiping me down doesn't win any points with me. Not at all because I know exactly where it's all leading . . . to their continued discourtesy of me and to my own unwillingness to speak up and talk trash to them!

Somebody help me! I'm real close to becoming a 'basket' case!

Who Am I?

WHO AM I?

I know that people don't care for me. I get that! I know, for the most part, that they're afraid of me, or that they just refuse to believe in me at all.

Stories flourish about me by people who have purportedly seen me and by portrayals of me that are often assimilated into 'media concoctions' which are then advertised to the public as being ". . . something only the brave could see . . ." I've been a real money-maker for authors and film studios alike. I'm often discussed while a group is assembled around a campfire . . . in the woods . . . at night! Why? Because people get a thrill out of hearing stories about me.

I don't like that people are afraid of my 'presence', but they are! It's that very misguided fear of me that results in one's preconceived notions and apprehensions and, oftentimes, ends up with their belief that they just can't live with me! Sometimes, a chosen one will gather together those seeking closure and will seat them around a table; have them join hands; and will then attempt to make 'contact' with me.

It's been theorized that I continue to be because I've not finished something here; that there's still someone here with whom I need to communicate.

Despite all these fears, some individuals, many as a matter of fact, opt to actually enjoy an animated version of me . . . one they affectionately refer to as being 'friendly'.

Who Am I?

WHO AM I?

If big is popular, then I'm very popular because . . . I am big! Unbelievably big! Five Boeing 747 Jumbo Jets lined up end to end would not be longer than I. It's been learned that one of the things that 'floats peoples' boats', so to speak is how big I am!

The popularity of what I provide is causing more and more people to be flocking to me. People do come to me from around the world, pretty much year 'round, to enjoy what it is that I provide. They stay with me for several days and then leave; satisfied, I hope. Others will arrive to replace those who are leaving and the process will repeat itself over and over again.

It can certainly be an exotic time, which brings me to these questions: What causes something to be exotic? Eating? Partying? Drinking? Just relaxing? Well, I can provide all that and more! I can provide it for adults only or for entire families. Either way, all will have a blast!

There are certain venues at which they'll have to arrive in order to get to me and when they do I'll see to it that they are well taken care of. Early on they probably had numerous chances to make choices of their own liking about me and in turn it's my duty to see that those choices are granted and for all to be satisfied. (You see, if they like me this time, they will more than likely come to visit me again.)

Perhaps you've already come to visit me and maybe you've already enjoyed what I've had to offer but, considerately speaking, if during any of your several days you failed to enjoy yourself due to a lingering 'Poseidon Syndrome', it's my hope that you will give me another chance to show you a 'carnival' of a lifetime.

Who Am I?

WHO AM I?

I'm a curious entity. I really am. I am well known but curiosity about me does exist regarding my continued seasonal appearances.

My origins came about many centuries ago when individuals would adorn me as a tribute to their 'King'. As traditions go, I remained as one and to this day my symbolism is projected worldwide and, has turned out to represent an extremely lucrative seasonal business. Conservationists argue that my continued use as a seasonal symbol is not eco-friendly and will eventually be the cause of my demise. That, seemingly, hasn't deterred those from setting up in that vacant lot over there and bartering me away, while they try to keep warm around that fifty-five gallon make-shift furnace.

I'm found during a particular season, almost everywhere. I'm found in town parks and squares; malls; New York City, (at a very well known location), and of course in homes throughout America. I'm even displayed as a national symbol right there at the White House each and every year.

Still elaborately adorned, my real fragranced presence and, many times, my beautifully decorated artificial counterparts, will stand as sentries guarding over the many items that have been placed under and around us; items that others are well disciplined to 'not disturb until that special time has arrived'. Sadly for us, it's just after that 'special time' that we become unwanted and, different members of the household will start to 'needle' each other on whose turn it is to dismantle us. It's a sad time for us all but we're counting the days 'till that special time comes again!

Who Am I?

WHO AM I?

OK, I'll admit it . . . everybody uses me. Some more often than others but I think it's still safe to say, "I Get Used!"

I'm a nationwide thing. I've been in existence since the late 1950's. I since have grown to be huge and most of the adult population, though they obviously take me for granted, absolutely depend on me. I'm relied upon, indirectly, to connect cities; allow freight to be moved; to allow you to get your family to Grandma's house; all without a schedule and at anytime you wish to go and . . . allowing you to be able to cover long distances with limited or no hindrances.

Hundreds and hundreds of thousands, even millions, make use of me year-in and year-out. I came into being largely due to man's love affair with the automobile and the vast distances the automobile could take him. I'm actually quite an elaborate network of governmentally approved design and usefulness.

When properly used and maintained, I allow for the swift and unimpeded flow of those using me but when I'm misused due to carelessness or neglect, I can become a nightmare for those who are 'bottlenecked' farther back.

I am, technically, designed to be, or designed to be addressed as, a 'North-South' or 'East-West' entity and am numbered as 'odds' and 'evens' respectively. My iconic green information boards are located at predetermined intervals so as to inform all of upcoming locations and distances. It's up to you to understand them and use them to your benefit.

You do realize that you can avoid most of that aggravation by just taking the next exit and using the 'by-pass', don't you?

Who Am I?

WHO AM I?

I'm not feeling sorry for myself when I say, ". . . people look down on me". Everyone, everything, has its place in this world and I'm no different . . . I too have mine. It just seems like I'm seldom thought about despite the fact that I'm such a 'constant necessity'.

During waking hours, sleeping hours, and all hours in between, I'm there. I'm there in every structure in every society. You can be certain of that. The basic law of gravity insures that I have to be there for your use and you do have to use me!

Sometimes I'm covered because someone feels that I am, for reasons of their own, otherwise esthetically unpleasant to look at. In some societies there is nothing at all appealing or appreciative about me; I'm just there. At other times I'm uncovered because my tones; my grains; my visible luster are simply too beautiful to be hidden.

I don't go anywhere but yet, I'm everywhere! I can't take care of myself but there are industries dedicated to making sure I am taken care of and . . . individuals will always be found who have the desire and expertise to maintain and enhance me.

Yes, I'm proud of me, despite the fact that people always have and always will . . . 'walk all over me'!

Who Am I?

WHO AM I?

I exist but am seldom, if ever, thought of as important. Everybody has one of me, or I should say, at least every household and business has at **least** one of me.

My location at these houses and businesses may be varied . . . but I'm there! My size and design may be varied . . . but I am there! I am labeled with numbers and-or letters and am accessed most days of the week by the ones leaving and the ones collecting that for which I am designed.

Sometimes the owners of me will have to go to a central location, a 'community spot' if you will, to access me. I'm a lot more recognized as being located outside of a house, but may very well be found indoors at many businesses. In some rural areas I'm located far from the houses because the distances between dwellings in those areas would make it impractical for one to walk door-to-door to get to me, so one would instead make use of a motorized vehicle to do such.

I know my owners appreciate me just by the fact that they come to me as soon as they arrive home each day or, as soon as they know the 'depositor' has visited me. They want me; they need me; I know it! I do think I'm taken for granted though.

Well, have I delivered enough clues?

Who Am I?

WHO AM I?

Got a house? Got an apartment? Then you, no doubt, have one of me. It would be a rare thing if you didn't and, in fact, I feel silly for having even asked that of you.

I'm not in constant use but I'm constantly there. You see me everyday but I'll bet you don't even know the name emblazoned on my top. You can use me every day but it wouldn't be uncommon for you to go any number of days without using me at all.

I'm going to be found in one particular room of a house or apartment because tradition says that's where I should be and because my 'certain needs' won't allow for me to be in any other location. I can be a dangerous thing if not used as directed and, in fact, have been blamed for many fire department visits over the years, even though I sit idly until otherwise activated by others. When used properly, however, I have an eye for reliability and am hard to be without.

Often, my use results in an aroma which triggers a person's desire to 'step up' and willingly satisfy a certain 'craving' of his or hers. Then again, there are times when the effluvium emitted from that which I am in the process of affecting, turns out to create just the opposite effect on people.

I am designed for practicality of use, esthetics of décor, and my location's available energy source. I am a well used and very important item and believe me, the heat can very quickly and very easily be turned up on this topic!

Who Am I?

WHO AM I?

Hi. No formal introduction needed here. You've known of me and surely have had many of me throughout your life. I should say, however, that those of the more 'senior' ages may not have always been on point with me but may well remember when I was first introduced.

I was first marketed by Gimbels Department Store in 1945, although quaint and subtle variances of me have existed since the days of Galileo. Generally speaking though, my own dated beginning came about because I proved to allow for a certain 'permanency'. I eventually became reliable, non-messy, and easily transportable by all, meaning that little 'well' was no longer needed.

I am something everyone uses or has used. Most people can readily access one of me although it's not at all uncommon for one to say, ". . . got a _____ I can borrow?"

I can be extremely inexpensive or I can be ergonomically designed and relatively costly. Either way, my function is the same; it's the people's preferences that differ. Why, it's common for one to buy an entire box of me for what another would pay for just one of my fancier brothers. You might see the President holding me when it's time for him to assert his power. He may use several of me at that time for symbolic reasons.

I must add that at times, though rare, I may fail and sometimes my failure will result in a ruined garment. I'm sorry for that but it's really the unlikelihood of that happening that really makes me 'click'.

Who Am I?

WHO AM I?

Doesn't it seem likely that one would gladly use something that is free as opposed to something that has to be purchased? And if that 'something' was free and readily accessible and one didn't have to store it at his or her home, wouldn't it be prudent to utilize that 'something' and seemingly have the best of both worlds? Well . . . it ain't happenin'!

There are places like this throughout this nation of ours. Oh, I get paid for but it's not so much . . . 'out of your pockets'. You each help to maintain me by your dutiful commitment to government but, with no real-time 'out of pocket expense', you can visit or access me any time you like. You can take from me and use what you take. You then give back what you took and . . . take something else. Wild, huh?

Sure, you could go out and buy that which was just mentioned but that's where the impracticality of it all sets in. Lots of times once you've used something, you have no further use for it. Now what do you do? You bought it so you own it! Well why not just come to me where you can use it for awhile then return it when you're done and have it cost you nothing?

I could speak 'volumes' about me but I'll just say I'm a place that can keep you informed, educated, and well versed. I'll allow you to sit back and unwind. Go ahead, 'check me out'; do some 'research' on me.

You could, in this electronic age, just go online, but previous to this age, your parents would tell you to just ". . . go _____. You **do** have your card, don't you?

Who Am I?

WHO AM I?

Hey, do you know me? Oh, I'm sure that you've heard of me and probably have seen me in pictures and drawings but I seriously doubt that you or anyone else has ever laid eyes on me.

I'm really big! There's only one other in our 'neighborhood' that's bigger than me but he's a real 'hothead' who considers himself a star! There are nine of us in this 'neighborhood' and though we might all be the same in age, we are not the same in size. I have neighbors but they're all 'spaced out'. One of my closest neighbors is referred to as 'The Red One'. 'Red' is quite harmless but has been portrayed to be otherwise. When all was said and done it turned out that 'Red' was just an innocent victim of 'science fiction' stuff.

My other neighbor, the one who likes rings, is pretty big also; almost as big as me. Those rings, though beautiful they are from a distance, are just a collection of old stones and dust when seen up close. Those rings are banded around my neighbor's midsection and because of that, he, who is so Godly named, is probably the most recognizable one of us all.

Me? I'm out here, supposedly, by myself, seemingly stationary but actually zooming along. I'm not dull though; there is a 'stormy' side of me, actually. And, a few years ago, I was the one that was in the news because of a series of collisions which were, miraculously, caught on film for all to see! I still can't believe they hit me. I mean, out there in the middle of nowhere and I still got 'sphered'? Is that what they mean by the "big bang"?

Who Am I?

Who Am I?

OK, let's try this one on for size. I'll try and explain myself to you, hopefully without giving myself away. There are a lot of me in the world and I suppose, a lot of me in some closets, coming in all sizes and colors. I'm sometimes necessary and sometimes not. I can be very plain or very decorative. I'm of various textures and can be made from innumerable substances but I've mostly been genuinely associated with a part of a particular, familiar animal.

Men use me an awful lot but women do too. Women probably have a lot more of me than men do so I can't say who uses me the most, Boys have me as do girls. The short use me as do the tall; the robust as well as the thin. They all use me!

While being functional, I am also stylish. I have no problem being both. Santa Claus uses me and just wouldn't look like himself if he didn't. The policeman needs two of me for two different functions and I must say, it does make him look more 'strapping'! Your dad no doubt had one but would find reason to use it to make you 'buckle down'. You would always cry and he would always tell you, ". . . this hurts me more than it does you."

Many moms, at least back in the day, would use theirs to the point where one would begin to wonder if they were going to be able to breathe at all! Lil' Brother always had one that was too long and it would be left dangling throughout his day. And then, after Uncle Jim finished his big meal, he would lean back in his chair, loosen me and would be heard to say, ". . . ahhhhh!"

C'mon now, don't buckle under . . .

Who Am I?

WHO AM I?

Can I have a few moments of your time? Can you listen to me for a little bit? I hope that you can because . . . I have issues!

I'm struggling right now and really, I don't see any reason for hope at anytime in the future. I think my 'glory' days are long gone! I mean, I like being in demand, being wanted, being picked up all the time. Oh, I know I'm still being picked up but let's face it, not nearly as much as I used to be. I've been told to 'relax', 'not to worry', to 'put my worries on the back page'.

Back in the day I was all over the streets. I was a tough cookie though, back then. They'd pick me up and throw me over the sides and you know what? I loved it! Oh, my exterior would be torn up and unusable but there was more than enough of my interior to satisfy all. My arrival each day was just like clockwork. I'm what gave "deadline" its meaning. People were clamoring to get to me!

I have, for a long time, kept people abreast of what's happening in and around their town and around the world. They find photos; people's concerns; humor and the like 365 days a year! I hold a wealth of information on each of those days but most people only want me for a fraction of what I possess.

I may have been the stimulus for your son or daughter's first job. Sadly, on some days of the week my own size made the job extremely difficult for most youngsters to handle. Now days that job is pretty much relegated to adults who, seemingly everywhere, have taken over the former duties of those early morning, door-to-door, bicycle-riding young people but hey, that's old news, isn't it?

Is my worry just a sign of the 'times'?

Who Am I?

WHO AM I?

I'm found in lots of places. That's not a real good clue at this time but your understanding of it will peak very shortly. When I say, ". . . lots of places", I'm talking on a big scale, like the world! I'm found everywhere around the world . . . kind of.

I, and my counterparts, pretty much rise up and stick together. We're sometimes considered dividers with vast distances on either side of us that are fairly flat. We're big and rugged and people look up to us. Some turn us into a playground but we don't complain, and that seems to signal to them that they can climb all over us.

Some of us are famous enough to be household names. Names that depict 'majesticness'! No one has ever seen us in our making, as far as I know, but there are those who insist that they know how we came about. That was millions of years ago! How could they know? How could they?

Some of us get pretty high which means there are individuals who are willing, and in fact, determined, to challenge those of us who are the highest. Sometimes we're just too much for them and they concede to that fact but . . . it also bolsters their determination which means . . . they come back!

At a distance, we're beautiful. Up close we're just too big for the eyes to appreciate. We are often depicted on photographs and such, thanks to the efforts of people like Ansel Adams and his famous photograph of one of us in Yosemite National Park.

Who Am I?

WHO AM I?

Hey! Where ya goin'? Well, wherever it is, we're going too! You know it's always been that way. It's never mattered where you were going or what you were doing; we were going anyway. We've never had any 'say-so'.
It's strange that we'd word it that way since we're unable to say anything. After all, we don't have a brain of our own, although we're real close to one.

We have our God given attributes but the one attribute that isn't God-given is our role in nosiness. We're a big part of what makes nosiness the heated topic that it is today. Oh, yeah, we're hanging out there picking upon every little thing. When we're at our best even a pin drop can't get by us. As long as you're awake we're sensitive to all that's going on around you.

If, however, you neglect us; if you fail to take care of us or allow us to fill with water or even if you start picking at us (we're sensitive, you know) we can fail you. We can become a real nightmare! You've been told early on to take care of us because once we fail we don't bounce back. Oh, you could invest in something to aide us but once the damage is done, it's done!

That would be upsetting to us and in turn could be upsetting to you so you need to hear our concerns. We can really make your world 'spin'. All this will 'ring' true unless you take-care-of-us! We're not just there to hold your glasses on, you know!

Who Are We?

WHO AM I?

I'm constantly on the move. You'd think I'd get tired and stop for awhile but . . . I don't. It seems my source is unrestrictive because my process never stops. I'm restlessly moving toward the middle of your world. I'm drawn there, I suppose, by gravity and or the laws of physics.

I come in different sizes and some of me that are large are known worldwide while others that are small might only be known locally. I have what life needs. At most times I'm teeming with life and all life has had to adapt to me and my characteristics.

I can become poisoned however by the very ones who are so reliant upon what it is I'm providing. All life needs what I am providing when I'm fresh and clean. All life suffers when I am not.

Aside from life's necessities, I provide for recreational uses. Sometimes that recreational segment is when my importance is noticed the most and all else is taken for granted. Eventually I'll reach the end of my journey and will collect to form this voluminous body whereupon the locals will immerse themselves and get great enjoyment out of what I've provided.

Almost always, somewhere along my journey, I am harnessed in such a way so as to provide energy to the surrounding areas. My power is enormous as long as I can keep flowing.

Who Am I?

WHO AM I?

I might be found somewhere downtown; maybe in front of a building or, I might be found outside or inside a sports arena. There are a lot of me located in our nation's capital and I am more than abundant in and around Rome, Italy. Most people, however, are familiar with me by seeing me in their own city parks.

I am art. I am designed to last for generations. Made from materials that are pliable early on but rigid and durable throughout my existence. I, and those such as me, have a need for being because of man's desire to remember his 'heroes'.

Oftentimes the finished object will show a martyr of historic significance, possibly mounted on his steed with one or two of the steed's legs raised. This is all symbolic in its representation.

But people aren't the only ones drawn to these objects. "Birds of a feather flock together . . .", many times right on top of the objects in question, with their 'deposits' often marring that object's often exalted and dignified appearance.

WHO AM I?

WHO AM I?

When I'm needed, I'm "oh so important!" When I'm not needed, I'm not even thought about. My job is to cover and protect. You say, "You've got to do better than that. A lot of objects perform those very duties." OK, I guess you're going to need a little more information than that, huh?

When I am needed, I'm needed in twos. When the time comes that I'm no longer needed it would be wise for you to store me and 'my significant other' so that the next time I am needed, you'll be able to find both of us, because we work together!

I do understand that there are times, regretfully, when an individual is physically handicapped to the point where two of me aren't needed. With all due respect to them I have to say those are the exceptions and that in most cases I am sold in matching pairs of various sizes, colors and styles. I perform a function but at the same time, I can be quite stylish!

There are those who are absolutely **not** handicapped who will be in need of me because their job requires such. This is most prevalent in the sports world where an individual will employ one of me to seize and hold an object until it gets transferred over to the 'side where I am not' so as then to be relayed cleanly to someone else whom, by the way, will be outfitted in the same fashion. This is a widely popular occurrence, especially in the US in warm weather and, in Latin America, probably year round. Can you catch what I'm talking about here?

C'mon, let's see a show of hands . . . do any of you remember where you last placed me?

Who Am I?

Who Am I?

Anytime one is performing a certain task they'll be looking for me, or at least they should be. I'm not hiding from them; no, not at all! In fact, I want them to 'see the light', so to speak, so they can benefit from me and so that others can benefit because of them.

Generally speaking, I just 'hang around' and do what I do, except on rarer occasions when I'll be found off to the side, still doing what I do but, out of the way of, oh . . . let's say, a parade. Either way, lines of people will routinely stop and stare at me while others, though giving me a glance, won't need to stop . . . this time.

I'm a colorful object and, supposedly, a lot of study went into my colorful design. My illuminated hues are purposely arranged and displayed so as warn and advise. It can be said that people have been subliminally taught to obey my three-toned variations.

I don't speak but all who **should** pay attention to me had better do as I instruct or they may be summoned to explain why. Sometimes people will defy me only to find themselves involved in a 'steel grinding occurrence' that often winds up under litigation and overseen by those who are responsible for governing such, and why? Simply because one failed to heed the internationally recognizable color for . . ."STOP!"

Who Am I?

WHO AM I?

Don't be hatin'! I'm here year-in, year-out. I don't know why people are so upset with me when I show up each year. I'm *not* anything new!

There *are* things I can make you do that my counterpart or adversary cannot. We both, as a matter of fact, can make you do certain things though the things on *my* list seem to result in a lot more consternation in people, thus making me out to be the 'bad guy', so to speak.

There is a good segment of the population that revels in what it is I can give them. Most of their excitement with me has to do with the recreational aspects that I create. Many areas of the United States and the world, as a matter of fact, cater to me specifically. Aspen, Colorado and Innsbruck, Austria are just a couple of examples of places that come to mind when thinking of areas where my seasonal offerings are appreciated. I do affect an otherwise huge number of heavily populated areas and it's that very population that curses me when I happen to precipitate heavily or punish them with my bone-chilling ways.

Many people, ironically, are living in the very areas that are most susceptible to my harshest offerings. I've always been puzzled as to why so much of the population congregated in regions where my impact is the strongest, when they knew that the conditions I would bring would be to their disliking.

I don't mean to seem cold to you, I'm just stating what seems to be the facts 'all wrapped up in a blanket', so to speak.

Who Am I?

Who Am I?

I exist in a variety of forms. I can be small, (tiny, in fact), huge, or anywhere in between. I'm an inanimate object that nearly everyone owns, or at the very least, uses and I, pretty much, provide all around enjoyment.

For you to 'receive' what I'm offering you, I have to get 'turned on'! I can really do my thing then. Actually, I can **only** do my thing when I get 'turned on'. But when I am turned on I find that, many times, you are too!

You really don't have to know how it happens but I'm the one that arranges for others to be speaking to you. It's totally up to you as to what you want those people to be speaking about but just let me know and I'll change from this person to that and from that topic to this. I do it so effortlessly too. I even arrange for people to be singing to you and most often this happens after you sit down and initiate the start-up of my host. I believe most of the song lyrics you know were learned from those who were allowed to 'do their thing' while you were concentrating on doing something else. When doing that 'something else' you were always advised to 'leave me set' where I am until you can find the moment when you can safely 'adjust' me.

With the advent of transistors and now, microchip technology, people have learned to transfer that which they want, after originally having heard it from me, onto their own playback devices. But whether they know it or not, it all began with me; with the family all gathered around me, listening to that 'golden age of _____' !

Who Am I?

Who Am I?

I'm found on surfaces where my presence there is all natural. There are those who don't wish to have me on those surfaces and will work almost tirelessly to keep me off. Those individuals and, in fact, most individuals, either want me or don't want me for reasons that have to do with their own personal appearance. It's called 'vanity'!

When speaking of surfaces, I'm referring to areas of one's body. Of course, areas of the body considered to be a surface will, a lot of times, be covered and mostly unseen by others. One area or surface, however, affords me considerable attention because I am almost always visible there.

This is the area to which individuals give most of their attention and is the reason for such a multitude of 'care products'. Products which are designed to beautify, cleanse, and manage; among other things.

Many of today's celebrities are adored partly due to me and there are constant attempts to mimic how those celebrities wear me. Michael Jordan, for instance, started a whole new craze on how not to wear me and Jennifer Anniston's style kept those, whose professional shops cater to the care of me, extremely busy trying to duplicate her 'crowning glory'.

Who Am I?

Who Am I?

I just keep happening. There's nothing at all you or anyone can do about it because I'm a natural occurrence. I appear, so to speak, everyday and have been appearing since the beginning of time. (OK, I'll admit . . . that was a bit strong for me to say that I appear everyday. That's just a little bit misleading.)

Still, people sometimes have a sense that something creepy is going to occur whenever I'm happening. I'm the primary reason why people can sneak about; go unseen; be so easily frightened. Sounds are more pronounced when I'm happening or perhaps, people are being more alert and more aware of what's around them, so possibly that translates into the sounds seeming to be more distinct. Either way, it's a fact, peoples' demeanors do change when I'm around.

Also, a whole litany of things wouldn't be needed were it not for me. There would be little or no need for reflective materials. Absolutely none! A lot less light bulbs and flashlights would be needed. The planetariums would be impractical, in fact, you'd never see the stars at all! And horror flicks? Forget it! It would take all the fun out of them were it not for me. Even at that, there may be some who would state that this would be a 'brighter' world without me. I think that goes without saying but I suppose a little more light needs to be shed on the subject before arriving at that conclusion.

Having said all that I must say this . . . there are those who are afflicted with total blindness that have never had the benefit of living apart from that which many of us constantly fear. That being, _____!

Who Am I?

Once Upon A Time

It's not that I was obsessed with her, but she intruded into my world and well . . . I did what I'm supposed to do! I am what I am! Hey, after all, the only thing I ever wanted was to live one of those 'fairy tale' lives.

I would catch sight of her just about the same time of the day, every other day . . . pretty much the same time that I would be enjoying my . . . "every-other-day" afternoon meal. She never paid any attention to me; in fact, I don't even think she knew I was there. After all, I was always several yards off the path that she was on and, as I was eating, she never gave me any hint that she was threatened by me or that she was going to be any threat **to** me.

She never seemed to have a care in the world when she passed me; brightly attired with that hood pulled over her head, and moving along the path with a sort of rhythmic-hopping movement. Each time she passed by she would be cradling some sort of container; a basket, if you will. I never saw her open it but during her return trip via that same path, she always carried it carelessly; sort of like there was nothing in it or, at least, nothing she seemed to be concerned about. Apparently, she had emptied that container once she had arrived at her destination, thus her indifference on her return.

One day, just when I felt that I was going to go meal-less, and with the reliability of daylight, along came 'Lil Miss Happy'. Again, 'Lil Miss Happy' was totally unaware of my presence so I began following her. She arrived at a rather quaint and unassuming structure that was nestled in the woods, and she began pounding on the entranceway. She also began bellowing something over and over again; all unintelligible to me, of course, since I'm incapable of understanding any form of vocalization. The entranceway then opened and just inside stood a figure, whom to me seemed somewhat similar in stature to the brightly clad 'Lil Miss Happy' though a bit taller and a bit more worn for wear. A more wrinkled complexion and a lot less zest in her step easily distinguished her from her little visitor, however.

Once 'Lil Miss Happy' was inside, the entranceway closed which prevented me from witnessing anything more so I settled in, just out of sight of anyone who might arrive at or exit the structure. There I waited and watched. I knew she'd have to come out sooner or later. When the entranceway reopened, out came 'Lil Miss Happy' and she hadn't lost a step! She left as she arrived; bouncing and happy! After she jaunted away, I decided to mimic her earlier actions to try to get the figure inside to again open the entranceway. I'd then run in and hopefully take advantage of she whom I'd witnessed at that entranceway. My plan was successful, though obviously unpleasant for her. Having satisfied myself, I sleepily slumped onto a wide and soft piece of furnishing and did remain comfortably in that reposed state until a loud pounding awakened me.

Absolutely startled, I pulled the heavy fabrics over me that were covering the wide, soft furnishing on which I had been sleeping. Only my eyes and nose remained visible. The pounding continued and I finally realized the source of that clatter . . . 'Lil Miss Happy' is out there asking to gain entrance to this structure. "I'm hungry, she wants in! I'm stronger, so if she **gets** in . . . hmmmm . . . ; this is gonna work out fine for me . . . just fine!"

Being unable to verbalize, I couldn't invite her in but she finally forced open the entranceway, possibly out of concern that the aforementioned 'wrinkled figure' had, uncharacteristically, failed to open it for her.

Once having gained entrance to my new abode, 'Lil Miss Happy' gasped and mouthed something and pointed to my eyes; upon which . . . I winked at her.

She then gasped and mouthed something again, this time pointing to my nose; upon which . . . I wiggled it back and forth.

She then pulled the fabrics away from me and with a look of absolute terror on her face, verbalized again, this time pointing to my mouth; upon which . . . I drooled and licked my lips! She let out a sound that was louder than all the wildlife in the woods and then, she bolted out the entranceway and oh yeah, I was in hot pursuit!

I was met outside the entranceway of that so-called "quaint and unassuming" structure by two seemingly overly aggressive figures, both running toward me and waving what appeared, to me, to be objects that could easily split the hardest of any tree in those woods. I could only imagine what those objects would do to me! It might not be in my best of interest to stand here and find out so I, all in an instant's time, analyzed the situation, altered my plans, turned and ran in the opposite direction. They were chasing me but of course with them running on only half the number of legs as I, their efforts were proved futile!

"Well, admittedly, 'Lil Miss Happy' outfoxed me or, should I say, out wolfed me? That's OK though. I'm sure other opportunities will present themselves and I will go on to have a fairy tale existence where I'll end up living, . . . 'HAPPILY EVER AFTER'."

CBDowney

WHO AM I?

I am very important to you, to everyone, though it won't sound like I mean it as you read my following description. I'm not for sale anywhere and I can't be manufactured. I'm not a medicine but at times I can make others feel better. I'm with you all the time just waiting to be used but at the most appropriate times you somehow still fail to use me. Why is that?

Another thing that you will be unable to do with me is to 'take me off' as you would your shoes or watch or hat. I'd love for you to understand my importance but it's hard to explain in light of the fact that I can't perform any tasks. I can't help you remember anything. I can't advise you or urge you or compliment you. If it's any consolation however, I don't complain or judge or point fingers and you'll **always** have me there when you want to use me. My only wish is that it would be often.

You're not the only one with me; others have me also. Everyone has me but many individuals act so stoical that I never get to shine. One shouldn't be so resigned, so resistant. Let me out! Let me do my thing!

I've been described as 'infectious' and when I am, all around seems to be brighter and happier. All need to realize that I'm that helpful little something that can easily make someone's day better because, ". . . when you're _____, yes when you're _____, the-whole-world-_____—with-you!"

Who Am I?

Who Am I?

I'm going to tell you about myself and when I do you're probably going to say this is all a bunch of 'fluff'. Hear me out though, because I too am one you should recognize.

I have a reason for being even though I serve no tangible purpose in your life. In fact, you oftentimes will scoff when I come by. It will seem like you don't want me around at all. I don't try to aggravate you, it's just that you're in, or I should say, under my path at the time I'm passing by which makes you think I'm purposely inhibiting that which you are in the process of enjoying.

I actually do have a purpose inasmuch as life is concerned. I'm not a creator of life but I do provide that which sustains life. I **can** be considered a 'carrier'.

I can be seen pretty much everyday and night of the year except for maybe in desert areas, where my appearances are much less frequent. I do get mentioned on that five minute segment of your evening newscast and during the continual updates on your radio programs. There seems to be a lot more positive excitement when it's revealed that I will be nonexistent in the coming day or days. That makes it pretty 'clear' that I'm far from being everyone's' favorite!

I'm sometimes gray and menacing and at times frothing with ferocity. At other times I'm white and fluffy and amazingly peaceful. On some occasions I'm said to mimic almost anything imaginable, but . . . only briefly because my 'form' will drift apart very quickly. It's just a matter of you lying on your back in the cool grass, looking up and imaginatively describing me metaphorically.

Who Am I?

WHO AM I?

I was just wondering . . . should my importance be measured by how much I'm mentioned? I ask that because I'm not talked about very much at all. Oh, I'll get some mention when I fail you, and at those times, mention of me will be interspersed with a few select adjectives of a derogatory nature, but that's ok. I get that!

I'm more likely going to be part of a garment and, a part of the deal when you purchased that garment. You may or may not have paid any attention to me at that time though. On the other hand, perhaps you **did** notice me because you felt I enhanced the look of your selection.

I might be of the bright metallic type which creates a nice contrasting line on the garment or, I might be of the more common matching colored, plastic variety.

I bring sides together. There are competitors of mine designed to do almost the same thing but who are, for the most part, unable to smoothly 'hide the gaps' as well as I can. I allow for that neatly laid seam and am quick to bring it all together although some individuals may have to 'suck it in' while they are, at the same time, 'pulling me up'!

I'm commonly found on pants, jackets, skirts, and sometimes, decoratively, on the back of gloves and, on women's boots. Almost all of us are emblazoned with the letters "YKK", especially if we're the metallic variety.

Who Am I?

Who Am I?

Oh, hi there. I was just watching those folks out there frolicking; having the time of their lives. That's what it's all about, I guess . . . getting out there so 'it' can beat down on them. Just look at 'em out there with their sunglasses and that sun block on their noses and cheeks. Yeah, that's just great!

I don't mean to sound bitter; not at all. I know that they'll be looking for me at some point. They'll seek me; they'll have to! They can only put up with 'it' for so long before they'll come running to me.

I'm actually incapable of doing anything at all. I have zero energy output and because of that my existence is totally dependent upon the very thing that they are out there enjoying. Ironically, it's when that 'very thing' is in abundance that I'm even more sought after and, in fact, even more defined.

I'm generally mentioned with reference to the outdoors. That being a time when those unobstructed rays are plentiful but . . . never, ever will my importance be stated. It seems that it's just understood that I will be there for them. I don't seem to be an important thing to talk about or to wish for but I exist and though they rarely say so, I know they're glad I'm here. I know, eventually, every one of them will be scrambling to get to me, to find some relief from 'it' and its relentlessness. Some will find solitude in me all day right here under the big elm.

In terms of who's more important, I suppose you'd say 'it' is, but . . . would you want to try spending time with 'it' if you knew there was no 'me'?

Who Am I?

WHO AM I?

Do you have that 'get-up-and-go'? Well then, show us! Get up and go! We're ready and itching to go! You manage to give us plenty of freedom as long as we're in the house; while in the shower; while in bed. As usual though, when you leave the house our freedom is gone! You hide us away and tie knots on top of us to make sure we don't get out.

As good and as useful as we are to you, we almost always get treated that way! OK, I'll give you that. It is true, in the summertime you do sometimes give us more freedom outdoors. When you do though, we're subjected to dirt and pebbles and sometimes, slashing blades of grass; and that 'post' thing that comes between two of my cousins; it irritates them to no end!

We take quite a pounding every day and we get hot and clammy and malodorous too! Of all the things we could have been, we got chosen to support your unappreciative _____ self! We just wish you'd give us a good soaking more often or maybe have someone give us a good 'rub'. If you'd do that it would make those at the end of us curl up with excitement! We'd actually promise not to make you giggle while they're rubbing us. How about that?

Who Am I?

WHO AM I?

There aren't too many of us left anymore. We used to be all over town and would automatically be included in a teenager's night out.

The young folks, teenagers and the like, would frequent us while on a date. We'd invite them in and attempt to hold their attention but that was a tough thing to do because much of their attention was being diverted 'elsewhere', if you know what I mean.

There were those whose job it was to walk around and make sure all was 'in order' in my establishment. That turned out to be a difficult job because the place was always so poorly illuminated. Actually, the *only* illumination was from up front where the planned so-called 'attention-getter' was positioned and its limited luminance was all there was to penetrate the cavernous seating area. Those whose job it was to patrol, so to speak, would have use of flashlights and would sometimes have to escort some policy violators out of the premises.

Ah, I'm not so big anymore and that's due, in part, to the prohibitive cost associated with me and the obvious trend toward the amount of home entertainment that's available today. It's nostalgic now days to go to one of me but believe me when I say, ". . . I used to be the 'reel' deal!"

Who Am I?

WHO AM I?

You won't be able to place me in any particular location because . . . well, I'm not! I can be found in the country; on a hillside; inside a small town; next to a church, or even in a big city where some historic significance has prevented me from being moved or relocated.

I am, for the most part, cared for and looked after year 'round. Those who 'stay here' never so much as make a peep of trouble but, vandals have been known to create a little havoc from time to time. Those vandals will sometimes take 'stones' away from here; away from where they belong . . . moves that will later be discovered to have been part of a prank upon someone.

My boundaries often include a wrought-iron fence; one for which I'm not certain as to if its construction was to keep anyone from coming in or to keep anyone from getting out. At any rate, I can't imagine why anyone would be trying to get *in* here!

My history is one of macabre eeriness and has been the backdrop for many horrifying tales, books, and movies. Some people say that they ". . . wouldn't be caught dead here!" I actually beg to differ with them. My serene setting will be patiently awaiting their eventual arrival. They need to be careful of what they say; they just might be digging a hole for themselves!

Who Am I?

WHO AM I?

What an ingenious invention I was! Nothing mechanical, nothing complicated, but a stroke of simplified genius just the same! I don't think I'd ever be considered a necessity and in fact, most wouldn't even acknowledge my importance at all! When I *am* needed, however, and can't be found, things can get pretty sticky.

All ages use me although the primary grade schoolers use a course papery variation of me, and you can bet, every one of them feels that they have absolutely arrived once I finally become part of their school supplies!

I come all rolled up, which puzzles me as to why I can be that way and still, once unwound, provide my designed function for the user, with no ill effects. I get ripped off a lot, after which I'm expected to 'hold things together'. I'll do that but when I do, I become invisible to the one who might be handling or inspecting that which I am holding together and that bothers me a little bit. Of course, I can't *say* anything so my frustration continues . . . not that you should care.

I can, however, react with contempt. I can fold myself over, rendering that length of me unusable or I can, and I like this one, break off early and adhere myself to the rest of me then watch gleefully as my user picks and picks, trying desperately to pull me free; sometimes with disgust, many times with expletives spewing forth.

Oh, well . . . let me dispense with the fun and go ahead and ask you . . .

Who Am I?

WHO AM I?

I really came into my own in the past few decades. Before that, families would be satisfied to simply be 'out back' in their own lawn chairs, under a tree. But after people laid eyes on me it seemed that they all wanted me at their houses too!

Contractors were kept busy with a backlog of work. Then home improvement stores began to spring up and home owners were being urged to ". . . build it yourself . . .". Before long there were kits and do-it-yourself books. That's when I started popping up behind a lot of homes.

Some designs were very elaborate, with multiple levels, fancy, angled-designed slats and sometimes, huge vessels of water inserted right into me. Homeowners would throw huge bashes for friends and neighbors, (with an investment in something that spacious, obviously someone had to be invited over to help enjoy it). I'm likened to a room outdoors that has been all decked out. I might mention, however, my usefulness is primarily enjoyed during those periods when one is more inclined to spend a great deal of their time outdoors, savoring that which is so warmly and so abundantly supplied to them from above. At those times when the aforementioned conditions **don't** exist, I become a 'catch-all' and am virtually ignored by the very ones who couldn't seem to do without me before.

Originally, I wasn't worry free for the home owner. The weather meant that there had to be constant climate fighting applications administered to me, that is, until those almost indestructible composite materials came onto the scene. Now those **are** trouble free, which makes me even nicer to own and creates even more fun **for** me, knowing that those on the other side of the fence are harboring such envy.

Who Am I?

WHO AM I?

Wow, I'm a little confused! People understand my importance but they seem irritated that they have to use me. They don't need me for themselves but rather for their one particular 'possession'. Oh, you know me! You absolutely know me! I'll even bet you've had some of my 'give-away' glass tumblers at some time or another.

I've been in existence as long as that so-called 'possession' has. That 'possession' of yours is no good without what it is I'm providing. I'm located throughout the nation and in some places I'm right next door to or right across the street, strangely enough, from another one of me.

I provide what your 'possession' needs in order to 'keep it going' and I also provide what is referred to as, 'other needed services'. My primary purpose, however, is to feed your 'possession' which will allow it to continue on and, in return, I will be compensated with an amount that is representative of the measured sum of the dispensed contents consumed by your 'possession'. This compensation amount has increased dramatically, even alarmingly, since my inception but what I provide is an absolute necessity to everyone with one of those aforementioned 'possessions' so, what's one to do?

There is a movement underfoot to reduce America's dependence on me by "Going Green". Are you kidding me? Whatever fueled that change?

Who Am I?

WHO AM I?

Hardly as popular as I once was but still a recognizable entity. Many of me are still around although all aren't being used any more. I'm sure it's interesting for one to see my quaint little structures during one's journeys throughout rural America

There are still some important and quite sizable structures of me that remain extremely busy; moving people from here to there. In some big cities I exist as this wonderfully massive structure of open space. The main reason for my being, however, is below ground level. From there you can pretty much be taken north, south, east or west on any one of our 'movers'.

But back upstairs, inside the 'big hall', you will hear booming announcements being made. You will see a big board that's ever changing as its tiles rhythmically flip, flip, flip to show a progressive roll-call of time and equipment.

Meanwhile, grab a bite to eat; get a newspaper or book; sit back and relax until the booming announcement instructs you to proceed elsewhere. Once seated, downstairs and away from me, you will be whisked away from 'here' and on to another of me. You will be attended to, in the interim, by a vest wearing, stub punching, aisle roaming individual who will be happy to assist you if you have questions about the next 'big hall' or 'quaint little structure'.

Who Am I?

WHO AM I?

Little kids are fascinated with me. They see me when they're passing by in their family car. What do I do? Nothing! On that day I just stand there doing nothing except looking. Tomorrow I'll again be doing . . . nothing . . . except . . . looking!

I wake up in the morning and go outside. I eat, then at day's end, I go back inside . . . to sleep! Whoa! Slow it down, slow it down!

I'm slow, I'm boring, I'm ignorant and . . . I know it! There are a lot of me but not a lot of variations of me. Oh yeah, I also only make one distinctive and recognizable sound.

Each day, sometimes twice, I'm brought inside where I'm 'serviced' by an individual who clamps a device to my underbelly and proceeds to drain me of my 'value'. It is a relief to have this done although the eager-eyed youngsters who are on their field trip are dismayed at the sight of me being 'pulled on' like that. But it is what it is so I swing my tail, turn my head and look at them with one of my big eyes and say the one and only thing I know how to say.

My 'value' is in liquid form and gets transferred to a huge tank and then to a shiny, elongated, multi-wheeled, noisy, smoke belching contraption that eventually pulls out of sight. If it's still daylight, I'm back to where the kids can pass by and see me and if it's night, well . . . you know . . .

It's a dull but easy life so I guess I'll just milk it for as long as I can.

Who Am I?

WHO AM I?

I am nearly everywhere but hardly ever noticed, at least not for my looks. Practically everyone has used me at some time or other, which will include those who use me for my practical and intended purposes as well as those youngsters who frequently use me as a toy. (I can be many things to an imaginative child.)

I'm pretty durable and am even given a number factor which corresponds to my overall strength and load bearing ability. Once I've outlived my usefulness I'm usually crushed or ripped apart.

My function is to hold numerous items that would otherwise be difficult to carry and control. I'm made from numerous layers that have been industrially compacted which accounts for my durability. But hey, don't let me get wet or allow me to sit for long in a damp area or all bets are off! If I'm wet and holding any contents, don't even bother to try to pick me up . . . I'll ruin your day in a hurry!

I come in lots of sizes and can commonly be found in your kitchen cabinet, your garage, a storage room or a warehouse. I'll bet right now you have more of me than you realize. When trying to count them you'll just need to be thinking outside the box.

Who Am I?

Who Am I?

I'm generally green or black. I don't know why I'm restricted to those colors but restricted I am. I am intended for use with an instrument that is dusty and powdery by nature. Me? I'm just hanging around awaiting the inevitable encroachment of that dusty little implement.

I don't want to give myself away so I'm a little hesitant to tell you where I'm mostly used. I can say, however, that once acted upon by that normally pulverulent component, one that is cylindrical in shape and very near the diameter of a first grader's crayon, I can be wiped fairly clean by the softly clad block which is kept on the tray at my bottom's edge.

Oh, yes . . . and for some reason, fingernails and I don't seem to get along at all! Some will cringe at the sound made by a fingernail being dragged across my surface. I'll bet you can imagine it just by the mere mention of it. Right?

OK, let's see . . . you, over there . . . come on up to the front of the room and tell me . . .

Who Am I?

Who Am I?

You might think I'm one bad dude! When I drop in on you it's with very little advance notice, and with that being the case, it leaves you with very little time to plan for me.

Oh, many have tried to understand me; to guess my next move, but in the end, and even though they are getting better at their predictions, I'm still just too hard to predict! Sure, it would be great for you to know my every move but until you learn to do that I'm just going to continue to threaten you and yours.

Individuals chase after me, photograph me, measure me, and try to do who knows what else to me and, depending on my ferociousness, I'll be called or identified as an "F-something." At any time I can chew them up and spit them out! I'm nothing to play with!

I'll come after you in the daytime, the nighttime, or at any time as a matter of fact and I'm impossible to stop. All one can do is to get out of my way. I throw things, I destroy things, I will make a sharp turn and destroy that which someone thought was clear of my path. It is what it is and I am what I am! I'm unpredictable!

I'm loud and I'm strong and my visits are relatively short. I'm ferocious and non-caring. I'll destroy, maim, and kill. All the things that you undoubtedly abhor about me, but you know what's funnel, I mean funny? The bigger and more destructive I am the more likely I'll be remembered. Sort of like martyrdom, huh?

Who Am I?

WHO AM I?

We're not widely viewed as being important. Our importance is normally seen or felt by those who yearn to employ us or by those who simply want to display us near their windows.

We're generally a large object, well made and often well polished whose purpose it is to entertain. Of course, most of my kind aren't able to entertain on our own; we need someone to be there to activate us.

That person will often find themselves activating a number of keys in order to 'wake us up', so to speak. The keys are always neatly arranged for one to select, and are most often chosen per the guide that's perched at eye level to the user.

We're non-electric, non-battery activated devices so we simply react to touch, that is, unless you want to consider the smaller, portable, modernistic models that are now available. Those *do* require an extraneous energy source and are remarkably capable of the electronic duplication of sounds that far outweigh anything we can do by touch.

Does any of this strike a chord with you?

Who Am I?

WHO AM I?

In the beginning you don't have me. I do, however, come into being within about thirty-five weeks or so. It's an unpleasant arrival because of all the whining and crying that goes on. It really gets old fast! Know what I mean?

I have several friends who are starting to arrive along with me; they're all around. Some of them are down there and some are up here with me. Some are alike in appearance and some are not. But then, after a few short years and after all that fuss upon arrival, we're forced to leave! Simply pushed out! All we were told was that we had to make room for a 'party of 32' that was moving in. That inbound group, as some of you from the 'cold-war era' will recall, were referred to as ICBM's.

People are told early on how to take care of us and if they would they'd be a lot better off later on. They're told to use an instrument that will break up that which is clinging to us. Many people don't follow that advice and eventually they have to visit the one who pokes and probes; grinds and scrapes; and often pries and pulls! Ugh! No fun there!

Eventually, you will revert back to your beginnings where you'll find that . . . again . . . you're without us. Can you guess who I am? C'mon, take a bite!

Who Am I?

Who Am I?

Oh, I hate to get tangled up in this one but here goes. OK, I'll say it . . . 'vanity' makes me a necessity! Really, it does! 'I am' because one wants to look better and to feel presentable.

I can be used anytime of the day or night but I'm mostly used after you get up from a night's sleep; when your 'something' is in disarray. It's my job to make it good again.

I do come in various styles, depending on your type of 'something' that is in need of maintenance. Men use me, rather quickly I might add, but women are my real fans! With my help, they pull and stroke and shape. They turn to their left, they turn to their right, then they turn again to their left and with a sigh of exasperation, they begin using me all over again! This is normally a time consuming endeavor for them but I do enjoy the attention.

They do oftentimes leave me clogged with that which has become detached due to my continuous stroking; stroking which has caused considerable damage. Hey, I'm just a tool! I'd have stopped had she allowed me!

Well, go ahead, comb through the clues to determine . . .

Who Am I?

WHO AM I?

I don't know how it came about that I should be included in a painting of a romantic scene and I likewise don't like the idea that at a certain time of the month I should be associated with any Hollywood type, beastly murders! Beyond that, I don't even know how I just 'hang around' like that!

I've been around for a long, long time and have not changed at all during that span and . . . I've always done what it was I was supposed to do. I'll admit, I'm given too much credit for some of the things that happen down there, but on the other hand lots of people refuse to respect me for what I really am capable of.

I've always been referred to as a person because someone, in their abstract reasoning, felt that I had a face. It isn't true but it is an interesting and flattering summation. I've been host to a dozen individuals and I'm a little disappointed with them for the amount of 'junk' they left behind. Hmmm, I wonder if they'll ever come back. I wonder why they haven't already come back.

Every once in awhile I'll feel all proud and dignified when I get people to look up and pay attention to me, all because I somehow got into a perfect alignment and created some phenomenon. Doesn't happen often but when it does I get all the attention I want.

Can you guess who I am? If not maybe it's just a phase you're going through.

Who Am I?'

Who Am I?

Do you think I'm a control freak? Do you? Well, I didn't ask for this job. I just got thrown into the mix of being the one who's supposed to 'make it all work'. Why I'm located where I am is a puzzle to me considering how vulnerable I am perched way up here.

Like I said, I didn't ask for this but I have the job so I'm doing the analyzing, the retaining, and the recalling . . . I'm in charge of all the commands! With that kind of responsibility you'd think I'd be of an extremely durable substance but I'm not. I'm extremely delicate and an injury to me can seriously affect any and everything else. The 'shield' around me is to protect me but it's inadequate for anything but the slightest of blows.

Science has long been studying me and is making a lot of headway but I still prove to be quite a mystery for them. If you had me in your hands you probably couldn't believe I possess the power that I do and you certainly wouldn't like what you were feeling. I'm soft and slimy and interspersed with folds and creases.

Everyone has me. All mammals, for sure, have me and a good number of other species have me as well. One can perform at an exceptional level with me or, can make it seem like I'm not there at all! I am, at least, the one thing that cannot be discriminated against because of race, creed, or color.

So, unless you're the 'scarecrow', you should be able to tell me who you think I am.

Who Am I?

WHO AM I?

Am I a great thing or a terrible thing? It's already known that almost all of you have established strong opinions about me. Some of you revel at my existence while others of you untiringly campaign for my elimination.

I came into being as a result of the Chinese' introduction of a certain incendiary substance that, once ignited, can be made to damage, destroy, and even propel objects. That very discovery has led to the invention of me! I have evolved into a projectile propelling device that can create devastatingly destructive consequences for whatever is at the receiving end.

I am now regulated in every state of the Union although some states are more lenient towards me than others. Some individuals are prohibited from having me while those who do have me are subjected to intense scrutiny by regulators. There are those who are allowed, and in fact, required to keep me at their 'beck and call' but that will sometimes result in renegade forces or even worse, a renegade individual!

Constant improvements, for lack of a better term, have resulted in exceptionally powerful descendants of the earliest versions of me. In recent times, 'control' has been the constant theme by those against, while adherence to one of our constitutional articles has been the refrain by those in favor. This polarizing issue has triggered some heated debates.

Who Am I?

Who Am I?

Most people above the age of ten know about me and I believe all continue to remember me throughout their lives. That's due to a loyalty that developed during their stay at this place. Everyone can recall some special bonding that took place here. Though the stay was relatively short, in terms of years, many of those that met here are usually long remembered.

Nearly all of you came to me to prepare yourselves for that time afterwards, when you'd be plotting your own way. Of the 'four groups' that were frequenting this facility, three of them could revel at the fact that they were higher in the pecking order than another. Those in the fourth group couldn't wait until their time came to boast that same privilege. This 'one-upmanship' has been going on for as long as I've been in existence.

Usually I'll be considered a rival to another like me and there will be frequent contested events of which there will be some strong alliances demonstrated . . . for each side!

The end of one's tenure here will be punctuated by a colorful ceremony after which caps will be tossed and eyes will be tearing. Nothing stops there, however. As groups advance, 'fresh men' will arrive.

Who Am I?

Who Am I?

I am so special! I fascinate almost all who walk up and lay eyes on me. They almost always have to pick me up and try me out. I seem to thrill them to no end.

What they see when they use me is what they would have seen without me but that certain thing wouldn't have appeared the same because I alter the appearances of objects. I'm used a lot by the military, the hunter, search and rescue personnel, sports and concert attendees and . . . by peeping toms!

I'm able to be adjusted to suit the user's clarity level and, as is the case without me, I allow for equal eye use. Those who wear glasses can also adjust me to the point where they will find amazing results with me also.

I do have a relative who *can* be small, like me, but more often than not is much, much larger and can enable one to visit places far, far away! Another difference is my relative's single optical piece. My duties are pretty much confined to much closer venues and I cannot be nearly as powerful as my relative due to the fact that one wouldn't be able to steady me if I possessed that kind of power. Technology has me to the point where I am now found in a pocket-sized version; one that is as powerful as some of my larger, cumbersome predecessors.

So . . . focus on the clues and tell me . . .

Who Am I?

Who Am I?

People often say that they wish they could be me but could they really mean that? I suppose it could just be a cliché. I mean, think about it, they wouldn't live a long life; they would be hated, and there would be constant attempts on their lives so it's just strange for me to hear them say that.

Today it seems as if we're more hated than ever! Back in the day a by product of ours was used to help the healing process by eating the rancid, decaying part of a wound. We still had to keep a watchful eye out for those who were intent on killing us but we were still able to maintain an air of dignity for having a worthwhile purpose. That was 'back in the day'!

But getting back to that so-often expressed 'wish', the consensus seems to be that if they were me they would be able to see and hear what's going on behind closed doors. If they were me they would presumably be inconspicuous to others because they could position themselves on lamp shades, on curtains, on a shoulder or, as the wish is so often stated, 'on a wall'. That's when they would be able to see and hear all that was going on. So it's all about nosiness with you people, isn't it?

Think about it though, your long lifetime traded for my short one just for the sake of being nosy? Please! Someone ought to swat you with a rolled-up newspaper!

Who Am I?

WHO AM I?

How about this for a life? I'm positioned in such a way that I can hang listlessly until that something happens, at which time I will spring to life and stretch myself out. I'm dull, unattractive and practically unnoticed in that listless state but I do catch more than a few eyes once I 'come to life'!

Many people who use me simply take me for granted; never-ever considering my intended reason for being. Others do recognize my purpose and value and will go to great lengths to protect me and to keep anyone from taking me away from them.

I come in all sizes and the bigger I am the more admired I seem to be. However, my importance is nearly as effective when I'm small and, as a matter of fact, more people have smaller ones than have bigger ones, whether they want to say so or not! Some folks will hold me in their hand and wave me back and forth then place me back where I belong until I'm again needed.

Our Washington, D.C. officials, symbolically speaking, have a really big one that they constantly wave at all of us and one of which we cheer them for so doing.

I'm known around the world and practically everyone around the world has one of me to love. There is one of me outside this world where it remains displayed in its most rigid state. My symbolism there is from the USA but it's representative of all mankind.

Who Am I?

WHO AM I?

Please don't look at me like that! You know I don't play! I tell it like it is all the time, as you should be so aware. So . . . if you're looking for someone to tell you what you want to hear, you need to look somewhere else!

After you stand there and look me up and down you expect me to patronize you, don't you? Well, guess what . . . I looked you up and down also and I'm unable to tell it like anything but what it is. Don't be hatin'! This is what I see . . . this is what I have to tell you.

I don't really care how much you stand there and stare at me; I'm still incapable of lying to you and it's nothing you can break me of. Even if you could break me you'd have to endure a similar fate as those who might walk under a ladder, or those who open an umbrella indoors or those who have a black cat cross their paths.

You'll find me, and I mean literally, throughout the house; you'll find me in the car, in clothing stores and the giant 'bean' in Chicago's Grant Park is a variation of me. You ladies are so drawn to me that you carry a tiny version of me with you at all times.

Reflect on the clues and then tell me . . .

Who Am I?

WHO AM I?

You guys are real 'users' as far as I'm concerned! You use me and my brothers; I understand that but if we're important enough for you to continually use us couldn't you at least extend to us an occasional 'Thank-You'? I, for one, am almost always mentioned with a partner; just like 'peanut butter and jelly' or 'fire and ice' or 'stars and stripes'. I'm often referred to as a _____ and _____.

You put me and my partner to use at a very particular time, mealtime as a matter of fact, in order to separate things that are before you. You may use me singularly in order to extract things from jars, then in turn use me to spread that 'thing' onto the floury, edible thing that you removed from that long, wrapped object.

After that point I'll be rendered unclean and I'll be deposited and locked, along with numerous other unclean objects, into that dark, hot water spraying, soap suds dispensing contraption. Eventually someone will decide to remove me from such so that I can then be compartmentalized in a drawer or perhaps even be put back into use. If I'm indeed put back into that drawer I'll reside with many other of my shiny kind. The exception to that would be my brothers who are kept segregated in a wooden encasement above me. I don't worry about them though, they're pretty sharp guys.

I'm just happy you gave me time to vent. I'm not asking for anything; just wishing that you would maybe mention me nicely now and then; you know, sort of 'butter me up' a little. Know what I mean?

Who Am I?

WHO AM I?

Not only am I needed, I'm expected to be there! I'm cursed when I'm not! I don't cost anything for being there but that which I'm allowing *is* costing something. I'm almost always located throughout structures and can be located even in the dark by those familiar with that structure's lay-out. You might want to keep some cleaning products on hand because after awhile my surrounding areas will become soiled due to one's inability to effortlessly find me.

Most of me are designed to allow or disallow for the flow of a certain matter. Some of me will allow for a somewhat restricted flow in which the full realization of that which I'm allowing is diminished. Some will use this feature to soften or to enhance the 'mood' in that particular area.

Each structure is required to have a master for me and my counterparts. This 'master' will determine whether or not we will be receiving that which we need to operate. People are shocked to find out that they should have deactivated my 'master' prior to tinkering with me.

Consider me a real 'turn on' who's generally covered or surrounded by a decorative, color-coordinated plate which hides access to my repairable components. Though I am still widely used, automation has allowed for a hand-clap to do the very thing I'm designed to do.

Who Am I?

WHO AM I?

I don't like being referred to as a pest but apparently that's the general consensus for me and mine. I do apologize for that but if only I had a real purpose then perhaps I wouldn't be such a worthless nuisance to you.

Though a nuisance I am, no one seems to be afraid of me. Even little children will happily chase me, and their parents will find it utterly amusing because they perceive no danger at all. They don't think for a moment that the toddlers will ever be able to catch me. But you can bet those parents would be immediately concerned if those little crumb-grinders did manage to get their hands on my so-often-referred-to 'filthy little self'!

Hey, I don't like it! I didn't ask for this! If I'm not being chased I'm being made fun of because of how I like to bob my head whenever I'm walking around, and I'm found walking around a lot! I also get sick and tired of hearing people ask, ". . . where are their little ones?"

I'm almost constantly stepped on throughout my existence in your urban world. I'm so used to you that I'll walk right up to you, close enough for you to kick me like a football if you wanted to. I'm rarely seen in the country but I don't really know why that is. I don't seem to share the same passion for objects that you do which is probably why I'm considered 'filthy' by you. I think everyone also frowns on me for doing what I do to that ol' motionless soldier figure anchored over there. By the way, what's *he* good for?

You know what? I'm going to sit up there on that rooftop with some of my buddies, and you need to understand that after pecking and continuously eating like I do, at some point I'll have to do what nature calls on me to do, wherever I happen to be when I do it! Just get over it but . . . don't look up while passing that building!

Who Am I?

WHO AM I?

Oh . . . come on in.

It's normally a good thing to have visitors. I say normally because I have them all the time but I *never* consider it a 'good thing'!

I share a room with a couple of others and we spend all our time together. We're unlike each other inasmuch as our duties are concerned. I know that 'the grass isn't always greener on the other side' but I am a little envious of them because of how 'sweet' they have it!

All three of us have visitors and generally I'm the first to be visited. My visitor will cause a near total blockage of light to me and will then try to entertain me with a series of delicate sounds before dumping his problems on me. Oh, I think I handle it fairly well although sometimes I'll have a little tantrum and reject that which I'm being given. It is funny to see them scrambling to try and correct the situation. They give to me freely but they sure don't seem to appreciate my enjoyment when I give it back! Those are rare occasions though.

I must admit, for the most part they end up taking care of me with a strong downward surge of water after which, "I'm good to go!" All in all I guess it's not so ba__ . . . ". . . uh oh! Here he comes again. I'm familiar with *his* routine; down on his knees, leaning over and . . . oh for the love of Pete! It's splattering! It's disgusting! Sorry, gotta go."

Who Am I?

I HAVE TO WONDER

I do travel a lot and during my travels I often make stops in hope of experiencing something new. "This trip and stop should be no different," I surmised. As I approached, it was beautifully illuminated; the blues and the whites, simply beautiful! It certainly looked hospitable. Admittedly, I still had a long way to go to before I could arrive there but from here it was absolutely beautiful!

As bright and beautiful as it appeared earlier, it was equally as dark and mysterious once I arrived. "A brightly lit area is always more inviting and seemingly hospitable," I thought, "but this is no time for me to pass judgment; I've got to see more."

Off in the distance I spotted some illuminants which appeared to be moving. They were tiny and distant but as I followed them with my eyes they seemed to be coming closer to me. As they moved from my left to my right the illuminants, which originally were white, were now of a reddish tint and seemed to be moving away from me, in fact, disappearing from my sight. That didn't concern me much at that time but as I got even closer to the area where I'd first spotted the white, then red illuminants, I began seeing even more of them!

These 'lights' were situated at each end of every one of those moving objects . . . white when one was moving toward me and reddish when moving away. Situated inside those propelled objects were anywhere from one to six figures, most of whom had their attention affixed in a forward direction.

I followed and discovered that those figures, those individuals, were quite disciplined! Each time their propelled object approached an area where a series of illuminants were found to be dangling from its above-ground wire harness, they would cease all forward progress. After paying particular attention to this phenomenon I surmised that they were doing so only when the dangling illuminant was of a reddish hue. When it changed to a greenish hue those same objects occupied by those same patient figures would resume their forward progress. I also made note of the fact that there were objects moving perpendicular to the aforementioned objects which would alternate their 'proceeding and stopping' activities with those whom I'd been following. It all appeared to be very well organized. While I was watching all this the 'line' began moving again.

I followed one particular object into an area where it came to a stop and the individuals inside began pouring out of it. They were all so jovial; they were all so excited, but why? The only thing I could see around this huge expanse of space was one enormous structure toward which some of them seemed headed. Some were waving some kind of colorful fabric on a stick while they, themselves, were painted up to match those same festive fabrics! They seemed to be a wild and scary bunch! Many more gathered in groups right there where their now motionless propelled objects were sitting and set up what appeared to be living quarters. Outside! Very strange to me but they seemed to be enjoying it to no end!

I went inside the huge structure and found it to be open to the sky but enclosed all around with the apparent attempt to maintain control over everyone's' movement in or out. The structure was gradually filling up with screaming, half-crazed individuals. Below, and seemingly the central focus of those individuals, was a huge rectangular shaped green territory on which were equally spaced sections designated by white borders and identified with numerical markings.

There were several individuals on this greenery and more than a few of them were attired in black and white striped tops. They were, however, far outnumbered by those who were wearing the matching, colorful tops with various numerals emblazoned to the front and back. They all appeared to look the same to me from where I was watching. I later realized that they were wearing matching head gear and when they were at the edge of this greenery I would see them take the head gear off and I then realized they didn't look the same at all! It is interesting to note that unlike the black and white striped individuals, these figures had, OMG, huge shoulders! Huge!

I've got to say that I was puzzled by the interest and anxiety being created there. I had to stay and find out what this was all about! I noticed that those 'big-shouldered' individuals were just milling around while those in all the surrounding viewing areas seemed remarkably calm, but once those on the greenery started to spread out, those same viewers began roaring and chanting and screaming at an almost unbelievable decibel level! But you know what? Those viewers remained disciplined and stayed right there in their originally assigned areas.

Down on the greenery, one faction, all attired in the same colors, would form a circle, so to speak, before going to their spread-out positions. The other group, also uniformly attired though in a different color, stood patiently and waited for the 'others' to spread out. There seemed to be two distinct lines seemingly designed to create a physical opposition to each other. Again, discipline seemed to prevail here because not one of those standing and waiting would dare cross what seemed to be an imaginary line until the opposing group signaled their permission to do so. That's when mass chaos erupted!

Torsos went everywhere! When an individual was pulled to the surface, and this almost always would happen to the one who apparently decided to carry something the others wanted very badly, the individuals in the black and white stripes would produce some sort of shrill noise and wave their arms and again . . . discipline would prevail! It was difficult for me to understand how someone could, at one moment, be standing calmly and patiently then physically try to rip someone's head off the next! This went on for quite some time and during that time each side often exchanged assigned duties. Some of the viewers were a lot more joyous than others and in the end you could tell that all were not pleased with what they had witnessed. All slowly filed out of the giant structure and got back into their propelled objects and spread out into the darkness via the various avenues.

Still being a follower, I found myself now in a savory smelling location where a great number of individuals were congregated. Many of those individuals seemed to be consuming things; different kinds of things and all appeared to be in a very contented mood. It seemed to me that there was a person there whose job it was to provide those who were seated with whatever consumable items the seated ones desired. It did not appear that very many of the seated individuals were at all acquainted with any others throughout that huge room although there was a great deal of conversing taking place at some of the singular seating arrangements. I saw some of them pushing themselves away from their booths and subsequently rubbing their midsections, and with obvious satisfaction. They weren't getting up to leave but the impression I got was that they were finished consuming.

Wanting to move on, I followed one of those figures out of this structure and into another, after having transported ourselves through a maze of opposing propelled objects and dangling illuminants. This latest structure was quite tall and was heavily dotted with glass covered openings. There was an expanse of space beside this structure on which was an accumulation of the, now idle, propelled objects. Inside I saw a series of framed entrances, all of which had numerals attached and my host, seemingly unaware of my presence, entered one of those. Beyond that entranceway I found the space to be otherwise unoccupied. He proceeded to an area where a large rectangular white box stood and he opened it. I was surprised by the frigid air that emanated from that object! Once having reached in he grabbed a cylindrical object from it and tinkered with its top until it finally resulted in a gaseous 'pop'! He put it up to his mouth, tilted his head back, and took several gulps of its contents before setting it down, after which he began disrobing.

He stripped down to the material covering his muscular frame then stepped into a cubicle and twisted a knob which produced a liquid spray; a spray below which he stood where he began rubbing a lather producing substance all over his torso. He finished by allowing the spray to free his torso of all remaining lather, twisted the knob to a point where the liquid spray came to a stop, then grabbed a large cloth to wipe away the very liquid that he voluntarily sprayed upon himself just minutes before!

After going into another section of this 'place' he donned a couple of garments but nowhere near the number of garments that he had on earlier! He then picked up a circular object of which there was a front side that was full of integers, and proceeded to tinker with the back of it. After setting it down he moved toward a long, flat object and climbed onto it. He pulled a fabric over himself and closed his eyes. It's my guess that this is his charging station and if he was anything like his counterparts I had seen earlier, he undoubtedly had used up a lot of his energy and was in real need of recharging. I didn't think there was anything that I could have learned after he applied himself to that so I decided to be on my way.

My journey has to continue and it will be long. It will no doubt be filled with other stops of interest but I don't think I'll ever find, explore, or depart from a place where I'll have as many unanswered questions as I did at **that** stop! The question I keep asking myself is, ". . . how much more did I fail to witness back there and above all, I have to wonder, where was I?"

Do you have any idea as to who I am?

                                CBDOWNEY

Who Am I?

Hear me out. I might be naïve or I might just be a little bit confused but, would someone mind telling me why I am like I am? I mean, why am I so skittish; so easy to scare? What has happened to me to make me that way?

I don't think there's anything menacing about my looks that would cause a person to want to hurt me. I don't think there's anything threatening in my nature that would make others feel unsafe around me. Having said that, do you know that I'm born 'afraid'? That's right! I'm afraid of people and the mystery is that I'm afraid of them the first time I see them . . . without them ever having done anything to me! What's up with that? Did my parents subliminally convey to me the danger I'm in because they, themselves, were subjected to some injustice by one or many of 'those', out there?

I can understand being afraid of people *after* I see them because I've seen some of them trying, and sometimes succeeding, to kill us so they can have us mounted and displayed in their trophy rooms. They sometimes will use that spring-like rod to propel one of those pointed-tipped sticks at us. Some will use that booming 'thunder stick' that we just aren't fast enough to react to. Like I said, once we've witnessed these attacks we have reason to fear for our lives and it's to our advantage to be wary. We know that 'he' will try to disguise himself, climb up in a tree, and use certain scents to lure us into a trap. We are aware of those tactics and we are wise to fear those things but, why are we *born* afraid?

Here's another puzzling thing: what is our stupid fascination with headlights? Can anyone tell me that? Why do we just stand there when those lights are approaching? Why are we so quick to run from people but continually refuse to get out of the way of those oncoming lights?

Who Am I?

<u>WHO AM I?</u>

Hi. I'm glad I've gotten a chance to talk to you because I don't want to miss anyone at all. I want to eventually 'get in your head'. I've always tried to do that with everyone and, in fact, have probably succeeded in doing so to the majority of people; at least to some degree.

I suppose I could be described as a 'mental thing' that likes to prey on a person's fear or uncertainties. I got handed down from generation to generation and seemingly nowhere along that long chain of generations has anyone been able to dispel me or calm anyone's fears about me. That thrills me to no end because it insures my continued existence.

Some examples of me might have to do with three people walking together on a sidewalk as opposed to four. Perhaps a baseball player or a manager going onto the field but consciously follows a set routine every time he does so. A person being careful not to walk under a certain apparatus; a mirror; knocking on wood; a four-leaf clover; an itchy palm; a rabbit's foot. There are too many to list here but I want to thank you for keeping them all active. I couldn't exist without you!

Speaking of existing, did you know that the building you work in has a fourteenth floor even though the building is not fourteen stories tall? Why do you suppose that is?

Who Am I?

WHO AM I?

Technically speaking, you can't see me but you have to know I'm ready to make my 'appearance' at any given time. You may have to be on-guard from someone who may be using me or you may, consciously or not, be using me yourself. At some point, I'm going to surface! I'm tremendously powerful and I have more lives than you can imagine.

Everyone has used me at sometime or another and many times it was for the purpose of gaining an advantage. As harmless as I seemed at the time, it was done, undoubtedly, for one's betterment. Many other times, however, it was found that I was absolutely unnecessary to have been used at all; that now it's going to be necessary to use another one of me to explain the previous one and this will perpetuate itself to the point where one will have trouble maintaining his original position or point!

A fairy-tale was written many years ago about a marionette that came to life. This particular marionette couldn't avoid using me and each time that he did so an elongation of a certain body part would occur. The fairy-tale culminated in a moral for readers to understand the dangers of my continued use.

I personally think the 'after-the-fact' distaste with me is way overblown. I'm just a little-'colorful'-thing that is commonly used and normally am one that can always be followed up with the statement, ". . . ah, I didn't mean nothin' by it!"

Who Am I?

WHO AM I?

I *am* real because I can be seen and touched and loved. I'm *not* real because if I were you would see me but you wouldn't want to touch me and probably wouldn't want to love me either. Your mom and dad would not have allowed me into their house and, 'cute' is hardly the adjective I'd be described as.

Nonetheless, children have loved me for generations and parents have gladly given me as gifts to their own. I've been made to look so cute one would have no choice but to love me! There are entire stores dedicated to seeing that children of all ages find me cute enough to want to come in and purchase one or more of me. They name me and clothe me and take me home and prop me up on their beds.

I'm depicted as a fun-loving character that you'd love to be friends with but it's something that could have horrifying consequences for the toddler who loves the 'touchable-me'. The 'absolute-real-me' is anything but touchable and the danger there being that the little ones will mistakenly think that they can walk up to the 'absolute-real-me' and touch and love me. Instead of being propped up on a bed, the 'real me' resides in the woods and will enter areas where mom's and dad's young ones are playing. *That* one will be looking for something to eat, not propped next to a high-chair while a little one is being fed. *That* one will make powerful grunts and growls, not just lie there quietly with that 'glassy-eyed' stare. *That* one will be hunted with powerful rifles, not cuddled next to a toddler in bed.

I am made to look like that one but it's a dangerous thing for children because they may think that what it is I'm representing is just as docile; just as cuddly; and just as cute as me. Oh, I need a hug, but with the 'representative me' . . . *not* with the 'real me'!

Who Am I?

WHO AM I?

Do you ever think about me? I mean, do you really ever give me any thought? I hope you do but I wouldn't be surprised if you didn't. Few adults ever mention me at all.

You definitely put me to use throughout your day but unless you're one of those slumbering communicators, you don't use me while you're asleep. I am making you use me right now, however.

You've been using me since you were a toddler, although at that time you weren't aware of my many rules. You've spent a lot of time learning my rules and perhaps have become quite good at your usage of me. I say 'me' but that's collectively speaking since none of the twenty-six of us are worthwhile without some others of us.

When you were about six or seven years old you began to learn about me with the help of a little jingle that had the same tune as a popular nursery rhyme song which referred to some sparkling heavenly bodies. Even the older folks can still sing the tune yet today. It's remembered because it helps them when they need to know what comes before or after 'what' in my group.

Those who are especially good with me will sometimes compete against others to see who can outlast who when it comes to correctly sequencing me for that which they have been commanded to formulate. One can become a 'National Champion' by doing this but it is nerve wracking! (Did I spell that correctly?)

Who Am I?

Who Am I?

I'm well known, particularly by those who are in need of an 'awakening' or a 'pick-me-up' so to speak. Americans are especially keen on that which I hold and carry around. Of course, not everyone uses me but I'm confident that all do recognize me!

I'm virtually a useless object, unless you want to use me to get a 'start-up-plant' going or perhaps to hold your many pens and pencils. When I'm normally used, however, I'm usually performing my designed duty. That's when I'm found being carried around by so many individuals. It's actually when they stop and visit any given venue that my usefulness comes into play. Sometimes I'm right there at home where I'm reached for just before he or she makes sure that all lights are out and all else is secured.

Only one hand is necessary for my management and you'll see them carrying me as if they think I'm trying to force some of my contents on their garments. Once in their vehicles they will place me in a previously designed compartment from which I won't be able to move. I'll have to wait for them to actually move me.

As previously stated, many places provide that for which my usefulness comes into play and one will have to pay a price for that very thing. There is one venue where that price is seemingly a 'little over the top'; one which is nationwide but found its origins in the Pacific Northwest; a venue where some individuals will gladly frequent in order to enjoy my 'yuppie' contents, regardless of cost. None of that affects me, however. I still serve the purpose, no matter what!

There are those who are never seen without one of me in their hand. It seems they have to have me! Oh, sorry . . . it seems they have to have what I *carry*! I'd better get a handle on things and ask you,

Who Am I?

Who Am I?

It's absolutely a wonderful thing for me to be able to communicate with you right here. Good for me, that is, because I know you don't ever want me to have to communicate with you at all, though strangely enough, my very presence in your home means that I'm expected to do just that!

I realize that sounds contradictory but that's exactly how it is! I'm just supposed to hang around here, seemingly forever, without ever communicating with you at all and you'll be absolutely satisfied with that, saying, "I put you here for the purpose of having you communicate with me but frankly, I don't ever want to hear from you."

I pride myself in being able to tell you something but because I don't get many, or even zero, opportunities to do so, I feel unappreciated. You will come over to me and 'push my buttons' to make sure I'm awake every great once-in-awhile but for the most part, I'm just a lonesome soul.

I can be very basic or I can be quite elaborate in my designed purposefulness. I can be made to communicate with you on one, two, or even three areas of concern. I can be designed so that I can communicate with and summon others at the appropriate and necessary times. I'm a 'protector' and though my value is enormous, it's said that no price can be put on that which I protect.

When kept up to strength, I'll be continually ready to advise you; even when you're asleep. Yes, even then I'll be right outside your bedroom door ready to 'speak up' and make you aware! I, ironically, will very likely be destroyed once having fulfilled my duty but, I will be praised by you and yours as well as by those brave individuals whom I summoned early on and who tried so desperately to save 'our' abode from total ruin.

Who Am I?

WHO AM I?

Hi. I exist because there always needs to be some sense of organization. No matter what you may be doing or where you might be doing it, there needs to be some sort of disciplined organization put in place. I pride myself in keeping to that theorized structure.

My purpose is to keep people together in a way that will expedite their movement from one place to another. Personally, *I* can't get them from one place to another but I can keep them congregated to the point where their point to point movement is, again, organized.

I'm located at each block while within the city but my intervals are more likely to be measured in miles when outside of the city. Still, I indicate to people that 'this' is where you should be if you want to make use of that which will take you from 'here to there'. In some rural areas I don't exist but the conveyance they are awaiting will respond to a wave of their hand. The problem with that is that any newcomers will be looking for *me* because they, naturally, wouldn't be aware of what the locals would call those 'opportunistic locations'.

Sometimes at these metro places, when several people are congregated and waiting, they will be comprised of both men and women; young and old; and you'll find this type of crowd during morning, noon, and night. Chivalry often exists here and many will courteously allow certain factions of those who are waiting to 'go first'. What you won't see too often, however, are the wealthy. In my observations the wealthy don't seem to be willing to be found in my area awaiting this type of conveyance. They will have themselves moved around by other means so don't bother to stop one of them to ask of my whereabouts because THEY-WON'T-KNOW! They don't need me and they couldn't care less where I am. A friendlier crowd gathers here with me, however; a crowd that can welcome all and share a smile. Honestly, I think I bring good people together.

Who Am I?

WHO AM I?

Not everyone has ever seen one of me. Not everyone will ever have a need to see one of me or even care that I exist. In times past I was an absolute necessity and someone had to maintain me, usually at some of the most isolated and treacherous areas anywhere.

If you lived in Oklahoma or New Mexico or Nebraska, just to name a few places, neither you nor anyone else would ever have a need for me. If, however, you lived in Maine, Oregon, or perhaps South Carolina, for instance, you very likely would have heard of me and would have well understood my importance.

I'm a dying breed but many of us still exist and many of us still maintain our usefulness to those who might be straining their eyes in order to 'stay on track' out there. I provide invaluable help with that although the modern day GPS has taken much of the 'value' out of me. Many times I remain in existence because of one's desire to maintain that nostalgic aura and their mere reluctance to just, 'let go'.

I'm not always a huge entity but when I am I seem to be more revered. I continuously have to have my surfaces maintained because the elements do serious harm to them. My real usefulness comes from the top of me where I'm referred to in terms of 'candle power'. Many eerie stories have been associated with my existence and that's usually when the ambient temperature and the dew point are close enough to create that seemingly impenetrable wall of opaque atmospheric condensation; a wall that my candle power is able to 'cut through' in order to give direction to those in need.

Who Am I?

WHO AM I?

My history, or existence, goes back for centuries. Originally crafted as a tool for cleaning, I somehow became associated with 'other uses' as well.

I'm normally referred to as a companion to another object; a type of 'pan', so to speak. The two of us go together. Historically speaking, I was the primary tool for keeping something clean back then but today I've been replaced by highly automated and reliable contraptions that do all that I do and, I must admit, those contraptions do it better!

Today, as was the case back then, I'm still found in almost every residence even though automation has minimized my usefulness and . . . I'm still pretty much constructed in the same manner as I was back then. The stiffness of my fibers along with those fibers' attachment to an elongated handle allows me to be used to maintain leverage over that which I am being forced to control.

The 'other uses' that were earlier alluded to include an instrument for certain evil factions of the population to 'ride'. That representation, however, so prevalent in past centuries, is scarcely believed in today. I don't appreciate that misrepresentation, especially given the fact that I've always been the one that was expected to clean things up. But, inasmuch as I insist on that being a misrepresentation, there is a certain day of the year when many young ones parade around in costumes and find reason to try to frighten each other. Year—over-year most of these costumes will change but not the one that includes me! No one has yet found a way to 'ride' me but the myth still exists and those young ones, and maybe even to a larger extent, those marketing people, seem more than happy to perpetuate it.

Another custom related to me has to do with ballgames; baseball in particular. When one team wins all games of a series it is referred to as something that is associated with me, and many of the patrons of that game will begin waving me in a celebratory and unified fashion. This particular custom, however, has nothing at all to do with my intended purpose and is only symbolic in its use. It too has taken on a life of its own.

Who Am I?

WHO AM I?

Say hi to all of us because you certainly know us . . . you **all** know us very well! We became acquainted when you were in primary school and there's no way you'd not recognize us even today!

In the primary grades you used a variation of us and I say 'used' because for the most part we were provided **for** you while you were in those primary levels. Once you were in subsequent grades we became a part of your own yearly personal possession.

There are many kinds of us but one kind in particular is the one that's most recognizable to most people. Our iconic packaging has hardly ever changed in all the years we've been around. We come in various packaging sizes and, the fact is, in those packages where our numbers are the greatest, the arrangement of us inside that package sort of resembles theater seating.

There are a basic number of us in the beginning but as you move on and, possibly, become more responsible you're allowed many more of us which, again, will be in that 'theater seating' packaging format. Some of us, regardless of packaging size, will be given more use than others and because of that we will occasionally need our coverings torn away. This is also going to indicate that we're getting smaller in size and, as a result of **that**, you may no longer be able to see our cleverly assigned names, which we always wear on our sides. Do you realize how difficult it is to have that many of us packaged together, where no two of us have the same name? Well, that's necessitated by the fact that even when you hold two of us together, side-by-side, it's still difficult to distinguish one from another so without the 'clever' names, you'd possibly mistake one of us for another. Of course, that difficulty only arises when we're in possession of that biggest of packaging!

Who Am I?

WHO AM I?

See if you can determine who we are by us describing ourselves. Some others have failed to do so, stating that we've been far too contradictory in our descriptions for them to be expected to do so.

Is it contradictory to say that we're seen by all, except for some who, for a specified period of time, in certain areas, are unable to make that claim? Is it contradictory to say we're seen hanging around and are seen lying around as well? We're criticized for saying we're seen as red, golden yellow, but most often, green! We're criticized but . . . it's all true! In those areas where we naturally come and go, we begin so tiny and green but soon develop into that full-blown partnership of magnificent color filled fullness!

We will naturally become yellow, then red, and eventually will lose our grip from that which we've been holding on to for the past several months. It's at this point when either you or someone you might employ, will have to collect us. This 'collection' will mean that we're being readied for a trip to a place where we will be introduced to conditions to the likes of a fiery abyss! Sometimes that 'trip' will allow us to avoid that fate but in so doing we will have to face a pulverizing alternative . . . we will be reduced to a 'state' of tiny, unrecognizable pieces for which we will then be packaged and sold to those who will, hypocritically, respread us all over their areas; areas where they, only recently, worked so hard of which to clear us.

Before any of that happens however, we can expect some 'little ones' to run through and even dive into us in their attempts to have fun. Afterwards we will be pushed and pulled together, usually near the curb of the street, and eventually that huge sucking contraption will devour us all and we'll then begin our journey to that aforementioned world of unenviable pulverization.

Oh, you'll rid yourselves of us but we'll have counterparts who will emerge the next time around and the entire process will repeat itself; sort of turning over a new leaf, so to speak.

Who Am I?

WHO AM I?

I'm just one of many; just one of a huge population. You surely know of me though you may not be involved with me and thusly may not know or understand the particulars of me. Speaking collectively, we would like to have a few moments of your time to allow you to understand us; to find out who we are.

We're not really indigenous to any particular area. We are known worldwide although one is unlikely to hear mention of our activities in places like Antarctica, or the North Pole, or the Himalayas. Areas of the like are unsuitable to us which obviously means we can be, and in fact are, considered a climatically desiring sort.

The lifestyles of our population are varied but one common thread of all would be that we are 'swingers'! The world might frown at that representation but that's what we are, 'swingers'! We've been so since way back in Scotland in the early 1800's.

Our times are spent traversing those specially prepared areas that have been set aside for us; beautiful, tranquil areas where we can 'swing' and choose the club or clubs of our liking. Some of those clubs are more popular than others and, in fact, some clubs are seldom chosen because, well . . . they just aren't that popular. We're all governed by our own perceived abilities but that perception is one thing; being able to carry it out is another! It's just not an easy thing to do! The one little object that we keep addressing, with the hope that it will culminate in 'perfection', is not at all co-operative with us! That's exactly why our time is so interspersed with so much swearing and lying. After eighteen of these 'redoes', however, we'll gather around and reminisce about it all.

The popularity of what we do can be attributed to those iconic individuals who have been able to keep what we do on the front pages, so to speak. Many of those casually but smartly attired individuals perform before a hushed crowd and at the same time are being viewed by millions more on T.V. on most Saturdays and Sundays. They've been the 'drivers' for this venture, creating and maintaining the interest that keeps this alive for all of us, whether we are athletically teed up or not.

Who Am I?

ANSWERS

9. A Baseball
10. A Shark
11. A Waste Basket
12. A Ghost
13. A Cruise Ship
14. A Christmas Tree
15. Interstate Highway
16. A Floor
17. A Mailbox
18. A Kitchen Stove
19. A Ballpoint Pen
20. The Library
21. The Planet Jupiter
22. A Belt
23. A Newspaper
24. Mountains
25. Your Ears
26. A River
27. A Statue
28. A Pair of Gloves
29. A Traffic Light
30. Winter Time
31. A Radio
32. Hair
33. Darkness
34. Red Riding Hood Wolf
37. A Smile
38. A Cloud
39. A Zipper
40. Shade
41. Your Feet
42. A Movie Theatre
43. A Cemetery
44. Cellophane Tape
45. A Patio Deck

46. A Service Station
47. A Train Station
48. A Dairy Cow
49. A Cardboard Box
50. A Chalkboard
51. A Tornado
52. A Piano
53. Teeth
54. A Hair Brush
55. The Moon
56. The Brain
57. A Gun
58. High School
59. Binoculars
60. A House Fly
61. A Flag
62. A Mirror
63. A Table Knife
64. A Light Switch
65. A Pigeon
66. A Toilet
67. Intergalactic Traveler
71. A Deer
72. A Superstition
73. A Lie
74. A Teddy Bear
75. The Alphabet
76. A Coffee Cup
77. Home Fire Detector
78. A Bus Stop
79. A Lighthouse
80. A Broom
81. Crayola Crayons
82. Leaves
83. Golfers

www.ingramcontent.com/pod-product-compliance
Lightning Source LLC
Chambersburg PA
CBHW021232280526
45784CB00005B/2066